Contents

21st Century

1) Who was Leicester City manager at the beginning of the 21st Century?

2) Who scored the last ever goal at Filbert Street in a 2-1 win over Tottenham Hotspur?

3) Leicester managed to escape relegation from the Premier League in the 2014/15 season despite being bottom in April, what position did they finally finish?

4) In what year did future England captain Harry Kane spend time on loan at Leicester?

5) Who scored Leicester's first goal of the 21st Century in a 2-2 draw with Everton?

6) Watford beat Leicester in dramatic fashion in the 2013 Championship Play-offs, which goalkeeper saved Anthony Knockaert's last minute penalty moments before Watford counter attacked to score the winning goal?

7) Which goalkeeper fumbled the ball into his own net to score a bizarre own goal during the 1-1 draw with Bolton Wanderers in February 2004?

8) Who conceded a penalty in injury time to give Liverpool the chance to claim their 2-1 win at Anfield in October 2019?

9) Who was manager when the club were relegated to League One in 2008?

10) How many goals did Matty Fryatt score in the season that Leicester sealed promotion from League One in 2008/09?

11) Who became the clubs oldest ever goal scorer when he netted versus Blackpool in a 3-1 win in March 2014?

12) How old was Mark Schwarzer when he became the club's oldest ever player in a League Cup game with Hull City in October 2015?

13) Which player won the Premier League PFA Player of the Year award for the 2015/16 season?

14) Who took over as club captain when Matt Elliott left in 2005?

15) Who became the first Tunisian to play for the club after singing in August 2015?

16) What squad number did Christian Fuchs wear throughout his Leicester career?

17) Who took over as permanent manager after Paulo Sousa was sacked in October 2010?

18) Leicester lost out on penalties to Cardiff City in the Championship Play-off Semi Finals in 2010, which player missed in the shoot-out after attempting to chip his penalty, only to see it easily saved?

19) Martin Allen was appointed as manager in 2007, how many games did he take charge of before leaving the club?

20) How many points did Leicester amass while winning the 2013/14 Championship title?

21) Who were the opposition and what was the score in Brendan Rodgers first game as manager in March 2019?

Transfers I

1) Which England striker joined on a free from Aston Villa in February 2000?

2) Liverpool signed which goalkeeper after he left Leicester in July 2000?

3) Callum Davidson arrived from which club in July 2000?

4) Which future Premier League winning manager was signed in January 2001?

5) Which team bought Neil Lennon in December 2000?

6) Leicester brought in which goalkeeper from Tottenham Hotspur in the summer of 2001?

7) Celtic bought which Leicester winger in August 2001?

8) Which centre back was signed from Manchester City in June 2003?

9) Dennis Wise signed for which club in September 2002 after leaving Leicester?

10) Which striker joined the club from West Ham in July 2003?

11) From which German side did Steffen Freund arrive in February 2004?

12) For which team did Muzzy Izzet sign for after leaving Leicester in 2004?

13) Which Premier League winning centre back arrived at the club in July 2004?

14) Which Northern Irish defender arrived from Lincoln City in June 2006?

15) Who did Keith Gillespie sign for in the summer of 2005?

16) Striker Carl Cort came in from which team in 2007?

17) Which two players were bought from Birmingham City in July 2007?

18) Iain Hume was sold to which side in 2008?

19) Which striker arrived for a second spell at the club in August 2008?

20) From which club did Leicester sign Yann Kermorgant in August 2009?

21) Joe Mattock was sold to which team in August 2009?

22) Centre back Sol Bamba signed from which Scottish team in January 2011?

23) Hull City bought which striker from Leicester in January 2011?

First Goals I – Name the clubs that these players scored their first goal for the club against

1) Jamie Vardy

2) Riyad Mahrez

3) Ade Akinbiyi

4) James Scowcroft

5) Dion Dublin

6) Yakubu

7) Leonardo Ulloa

8) David Nugent

9) Paul Dickov

10) Les Ferdinand

11) Wes Morgan

12) Danny Drinkwater

13) Andy King

Red Cards

1) Who saw red during the 4-0 loss to Arsenal in August 2001 following a clash with Patrick Vieira?

2) Who was sent off after receiving two yellows in the 0-0 draw away to Chelsea in January 2018?

3) Leicester managed to claim a 1-1 draw away at Brighton in November 2018 despite which player being sent off when the foxes were 1-0 down?

4) Who was red carded in the 3-0 loss to Sheffield United in their April 2008 Championship meeting?

5) Which two players were sent off during the 2-0 home loss to Birmingham in December 2003?

6) Who was dismissed during the 2-0 loss to Birmingham City in the Championship in October 2011?

7) Wilfred Ndidi received two yellow cards, the second for a dive, against which team in a 3-0 home defeat in December 2017?

8) Nikos Dabizas was sent off in the 2-2 draw with which team in the Championship in March 2005?

9) Who was dismissed during the Championship game with Hull in March 2012?

10) Which player was dismissed in injury time in the January 2015 1-0 win over Aston Villa?

11) Which player received a red card in the 2-1 defeat to Aston Villa in December 2014, although the sending off was later rescinded?

12) Wes Morgan was sent off for a foul on which Liverpool player in the 3-1 defeat in December 2014?

13) Leicester secured a dramatic 2-1 win away at Burnley in March 2019 despite Harry Maguire being sent off inside the first five minutes, who scored the late winner for the foxes?

14) Who was dismissed for picking up two bookings during the 0-0 draw away to Wolves in February 2020?

Memorable Goals

1) Which player hit a volley from the edge of the box against Liverpool at Anfield in January 2015 as Leicester fought back to claim a 2-2 draw?

2) Lilian Nalis scored a stunning left footed volley from long-range against which team in September 2003?

3) Which striker produced a chest control, then volley in the same match?

4) Jamie Vardy scored the Premier League 2017/18 goal of the season for his left-footed volley in March 2018 versus which side?

5) Muzzy Izzet hit a spectacular overhead kick from the edge of the box in a November 2002 First Division encounter with who?

6) Danny Drinkwater hit a volley from outside of the box in a 3-1 win versus which team in the first game after Claudio Ranieri left the club?

7) Leicester were relegated in May 2004 after a 2-2 draw away at Charlton, but who had given the foxes the lead with an audacious lob with the outside of his right foot?

8) Wilfred Ndidi scored with a powerful effort from long-range against which team in April 2017?

9) Stan Collymore hit a hat-trick, including a stunning volley, on his home debut in March 2000, but who were the opposition for the 5-2 win?

10) Who scored the only goal with a dipping left foot volley in the win over West Ham in April 2015?

11) Jamie Vardy scored with a lob from outside the box in August 2019 against which opposition?

Memorable Games

1) Leicester thrashed Southampton 9-0 in October 2019, which five players scored for the foxes that night?

2) Leicester threw away a 3-0 lead away from home to lose 4-3 against which team in October 2003?

3) Leicester broke the 100 point barrier in the Championship in the 2013/14 season by beating which team 1-0 on the last day?

4) Manchester City were beaten 2-1 on Boxing Day 2018, which two players scored for the foxes?

5) Leicester came back to beat Manchester United 5-3 in September 2014, who scored his first goal for the club that day?

6) Steve Howard scored deep into injury time to secure a 1-0 win over which team in League One in April 2009?

7) Which team did Leicester hammer 6-0 in the Championship in November 2012?

8) Who scored twice on his debut as Huddersfield were beaten 6-1 on New Year's Day 2013?

9) Leicester were humbled by a 6-1 home defeat to which team in May 2017?

10) Who scored in the last minute as Leicester beat West Brom 3-2 away from home to boost their survival chances in April 2015?

Transfers II

1) From where did Leicester sign Kasper Schmeichel in June 2011?

2) Which central midfielder arrived at the club from Manchester United in January 2012?

3) Future title winning captain Wes Morgan was signed from which club in January 2012?

4) May 2012 saw the arrival of Jamie Vardy who was bought from which team?

5) Striker Chris Wood was transferred from which side in January 2013?

6) Defender Matt Mills left the club to sign for which team in July 2012?

7) From which French side was Riyad Mahrez bought in January 2014?

8) Which striker arrived on a free from Crystal Palace in January 2014?

9) Which striker left Leicester in July 2013 to sign for Bolton Wanderers?

10) From which Italian side was Esteban Cambiasso signed in the summer of 2014?

11) Which future title winning right back arrived from QPR in August 2014?

12) From where was Robert Huth bought in June 2015?

13) Striker Shinji Okazaki came in from which German club in 2015?

14) Which central midfielder was brought in from Napoli in August 2015?

15) Who did David Nugent sign for after leaving Leicester in 2015?

16) Jeffrey Schlupp was sold to which team in the January transfer window of 2017?

17) Which centre back was bought from Hull City in June 2017?

18) Ricardo Pereira joined the club from which Portuguese side in June 2018?

19) Ron-Robert Zieler left Leicester in July 2017, joining which German team?

20) Which player was bought from Freiburg in the summer of 2018?

21) Who was sold to Villarreal in January 2019?

22) Which midfielder arrived from Monaco in July 2019?

23) From which Italian side was Dennis Praet bought in the summer of 2019?

Cup Games

1) Leicester won the League Cup in the year 2000 after winning 2-1 over Tranmere Rovers thanks to a brace from which player?

2) Wycombe shocked Leicester in the 2001 FA Cup Quarter Final when which player scored a late winner for the lower league side?

3) Who hit a hat-trick as Leicester hammered Nottingham Forest 4-0 in the FA Cup Third Round in January 2012?

4) Which team beat Leicester 6-0 in the League Cup Third Round in October 2001?

5) Who scored the late winner as Manchester United beat the foxes 2-1 in the 2016 Community Shield?

6) Which side knocked Leicester out of the 2000/01 UEFA Cup in the First Round?

7) Who opened the scoring in Leicester's opening game of the 2016/17 Champions League Group Stage versus Club Brugge?

8) Which team did Leicester knock out at the Last 16 stage of the 2016/17 Champions League?

9) Leicester lost 9-8 on penalties to which side in the 2011/12 League Cup Third Round?

10) Which team beat Leicester on aggregate in the 2019/20 League Cup Semi Final?

11) Which lower league side beat Leicester in the Third Round of the FA Cup in 2019?

12) Leicester were beaten on penalties in the Quarter Finals of the League Cup in both 2017 and 2018 by which team?

First Goals II

1) Ben Chilwell

2) Harry Maguire

3) Kelechi Iheanacho

4) Youri Tielemans

5) James Maddison

6) Matty Fryatt

7) Matt Oakley

8) Steve Howard

9) Lloyd Dyer

10) Darius Vassell

11) Marc Albrighton

12) Hamza Choudhury

13) James Justin

Premier League Title

1) Who scored the equaliser for Chelsea to secure a 2-2 draw with Tottenham in May 2016 which handed the Premier League title to Leicester?

2) Who scored Leicester's goal as they secured an important 1-1 draw at Old Trafford in May 2016?

3) Who headed in the winner as Spurs were beaten 1-0 away from home in January?

4) Who inflicted Leicester's first loss on them in September 2015?

5) Leicester beat Newcastle 1-0 in March 2016, who scored the only goal of the game with an overhead kick?

6) Who was sent off in the dramatic 2-1 loss to Arsenal in February 2016?

7) Who scored the February 2016 goal of the month against Liverpool?

8) Jamie Vardy scored in 11 Premier League games in a row by netting against Manchester United, but who provided the assist?

9) Who scored a brace in the 3-1 win away at Manchester City in February 2016?

10) Which player netted the late equaliser for Leicester from the penalty spot against West Ham after Jamie Vardy had been sent off in April 2016?

11) Which player scored a late winner on his Leicester debut in the 3-2 comeback win over Aston Villa in September 2015?

12) Which team did Leicester face in their last home game of the 2015/16 season?

21st Century – Answers

1) Who was Leicester City manager at the beginning of the 21st Century?
Martin O'Neill

2) Who scored the last ever goal at Filbert Street in a 2-1 win over Tottenham Hotspur?
Matt Piper

3) Leicester managed to escape relegation from the Premier League in the 2014/15 season despite being bottom in April, what position did they finally finish?
14th

4) In what year did future England captain Harry Kane spend time on loan at Leicester?
2013

5) Who scored Leicester's first goal of the 21st Century in a 2-2 draw with Everton?
Matt Elliott

6) Watford beat Leicester in dramatic fashion in the 2013 Championship Play-offs, which goalkeeper saved Anthony Knockaert's last minute penalty moments before Watford counter attacked to score the winning goal?
Manuel Almunia

7) Which goalkeeper fumbled the ball into his own net to score a bizarre own goal during the 1-1 draw with Bolton Wanderers in February 2004?
Ian Walker

8) Who conceded a penalty in injury time to give Liverpool the chance to claim their 2-1 win at Anfield in October 2019?
Marc Albrighton

9) Who was manager when the club were relegated to League One in 2008?
Ian Holloway

10) How many goals did Matty Fryatt score in the season that Leicester sealed promotion from League One in 2008/09?

27

11) Who became the clubs oldest ever goal scorer when he netted versus Blackpool in a 3-1 win in March 2014?

Kevin Phillips

12) How old was Mark Schwarzer when he became the club's oldest ever player in a League Cup game with Hull City in October 2015?

43

13) Which player won the Premier League PFA Player of the Year award for the 2015/16 season?

Riyad Mahrez

14) Who took over as club captain when Matt Elliott left in 2005?

Danny Tiatto

15) Who became the first Tunisian to play for the club after singing in August 2015?
Yohan Benalouane

16) What squad number did Christian Fuchs wear throughout his Leicester career?
28

17) Who took over as permanent manager after Paulo Sousa was sacked in October 2010?
Sven-Goran Eriksson

18) Leicester lost out on penalties to Cardiff City in the Championship Play-off Semi Finals in 2010, which player missed in the shoot-out after attempting to chip his penalty, only to see it easily saved?
Yann Kermorgant

19) Martin Allen was appointed as manager in 2007, how many games did he take charge of before leaving the club?
Four

20) How many points did Leicester amass while winning the 2013/14 Championship title?
102

21) Who were the opposition and what was the score in Brendan Rodgers first game as manager in March 2019?
Watford 2-1 Leicester

Transfers I – Answers

1) Which England striker joined on a free from Aston Villa in February 2000?
Stan Collymore

2) Liverpool signed which goalkeeper after he left Leicester in July 2000?
Pegguy Arphexad

3) Callum Davidson arrived from which club in July 2000?
Blackburn Rovers

4) Which future Premier League winning manager was signed in January 2001?
Roberto Mancini

5) Which team bought Neil Lennon in December 2000?
Celtic

6) Leicester brought in which goalkeeper from Tottenham Hotspur in the summer of 2001?
Ian Walker

7) Celtic bought which Leicester winger in August 2001?
Steve Guppy

8) Which centre back was signed from Manchester City in June 2003?
Steve Howey

9) Dennis Wise signed for which club in September 2002 after leaving Leicester?
Millwall

10) Which striker joined the club from West Ham in July 2003?
Les Ferdinand

11) From which German side did Steffen Freund arrive in February 2004?
Kaiserslautern

12) For which team did Muzzy Izzet sign for after leaving Leicester in 2004?
Birmingham City

13) Which Premier League winning centre back arrived at the club in July 2004?
Martin Keown

14) Which Northern Irish defender arrived from Lincoln City in June 2006?
Gareth McAuley

15) Who did Keith Gillespie sign for in the summer of 2005?
Sheffield United

16) Striker Carl Cort came in from which team in 2007?
Wolverhampton Wanderers

17) Which two players were bought from Birmingham City in July 2007?
Stephen Clemence and DJ Campbell

18) Iain Hume was sold to which side in 2008?
Barnsley

19) Which striker arrived for a second spell at the club in August 2008?
Paul Dickov

20) From which club did Leicester sign Yann Kermorgant in August 2009?
Reims

21) Joe Mattock was sold to which team in August 2009?
West Brom

22) Centre back Sol Bamba signed from which Scottish team in January 2011?
Hibernian

23) Hull City bought which striker from Leicester in January 2011?
Matty Fryatt

First Goals I – Answers

1) Jamie Vardy
   Torquay United

2) Riyad Mahrez
   Nottingham Forest

3) Ade Akinbiyi
   Ipswich Town

4) James Scowcroft
   Aston Villa

5) Dion Dublin
   Rotherham United

6) Yakubu
   Preston North End

7) Leonardo Ulloa
   Everton

8) David Nugent
   Bristol City

9) Paul Dickov
   Blackburn Rovers

10) Les Ferdinand
    Southampton

11) Wes Morgan
    Peterborough

12) Danny Drinkwater
    Doncaster Rovers

13) Andy King
    Southampton

Red Cards – Answers

1) Who saw red during the 4-0 loss to Arsenal in August 2001 following a clash with Patrick Vieira?
Dennis Wise

2) Who was sent off after receiving two yellows in the 0-0 draw away to Chelsea in January 2018?
Ben Chilwell

3) Leicester managed to claim a 1-1 draw away at Brighton in November 2018 despite which player being sent off when the foxes were 1-0 down?
James Maddison

4) Who was red carded in the 3-0 loss to Sheffield United in their April 2008 Championship meeting?
Patrick Kisnorbo

5) Which two players were sent off during the 2-0 home loss to Birmingham in December 2003?
Matt Elliott and Ian Walker

6) Who was dismissed during the 2-0 loss to Birmingham City in the Championship in October 2011?
Matt Mills

7) Wilfred Ndidi received two yellow cards, the second for a dive, against which team in a 3-0 home defeat in December 2017?
Crystal Palace

8) Nikos Dabizas was sent off in the 2-2 draw with which team in the Championship in March 2005?
West Ham

9) Who was dismissed during the Championship game with Hull in March 2012?
Neil Danns

10) Which player was dismissed in injury time in the January 2015 1-0 win over Aston Villa?
Matty James

11) Which player received a red card in the 2-1 defeat to Aston Villa in December 2014, although the sending off was later rescinded?
Paul Konchesky

12) Wes Morgan was sent off for a foul on which Liverpool player in the 3-1 defeat in December 2014?
Rickie Lambert

13) Leicester secured a dramatic 2-1 win away at Burnley in March 2019 despite Harry Maguire being sent off inside the first five minutes, who scored the late winner for the foxes?
Wes Morgan

14) Who was dismissed for picking up two bookings during the 0-0 draw away to Wolves in February 2020?
Hamza Choudhury

Memorable Goals – Answers

1) Which player hit a volley from the edge of the box against Liverpool at Anfield in January 2015 as Leicester fought back to claim a 2-2 draw?
David Nugent

2) Lilian Nalis scored a stunning left footed volley from long-range against which team in September 2003?
Leeds United

3) Which striker produced a chest control, then volley in the same match?
Paul Dickov

4) Jamie Vardy scored the Premier League 2017/18 goal of the season for his left-footed volley in March 2018 versus which side?
West Brom

5) Muzzy Izzet hit a spectacular overhead kick from the edge of the box in a November 2002 First Division encounter with who?
Grimsby Town

6) Danny Drinkwater hit a volley from outside of the box in a 3-1 win versus which team in the first game after Claudio Ranieri left the club?
Liverpool

7) Leicester were relegated in May 2004 after a 2-2 draw away at Charlton, but who had given the foxes the lead with an audacious lob with the outside of his right foot?
Marcus Bent

8) Wilfred Ndidi scored with a powerful effort from long-range against which team in April 2017?
Stoke City

9) Stan Collymore hit a hat-trick, including a stunning volley, on his home debut in March 2000, but who were the opposition for the 5-2 win?
Sunderland

10) Who scored the only goal with a dipping left foot volley in the win over West Ham in April 2015?
Esteban Cambiasso

11) Jamie Vardy scored with a lob from outside the box in August 2019 against which opposition?
Bournemouth

Memorable Games – Answers

1) Leicester thrashed Southampton 9-0 in October 2019, which five players scored for the foxes that night?
Ben Chilwell, Youri Tielemans, Ayoze Perez, Jamie Vardy and James Maddison

2) Leicester threw away a 3-0 lead away from home to lose 4-3 against which team in October 2003?
Wolverhampton Wanderers

3) Leicester broke the 100 point barrier in the Championship in the 2013/14 season by beating which team 1-0 on the last day?
Doncaster Rovers

4) Manchester City were beaten 2-1 on Boxing Day 2018, which two players scored for the foxes?
Marc Albrighton and Ricardo Pereira

5) Leicester came back to beat Manchester United 5-3 in September 2014, who scored his first goal for the club that day?
Esteban Cambiasso

6) Steve Howard scored deep into injury time to secure a 1-0 win over which team in League One in April 2009?
Leeds United

7) Which team did Leicester hammer 6-0 in the Championship in November 2012?
Ipswich Town

8) Who scored twice on his debut as Huddersfield were beaten 6-1 on New Year's Day 2013?
Chris Wood

9) Leicester were humbled by a 6-1 home defeat to which team in May 2017?
Tottenham Hotspur

10) Who scored in the last minute as Leicester beat West Brom 3-2 away from home to boost their survival chances in April 2015?
Jamie Vardy

Transfers II – Answers

1) From where did Leicester sign Kasper Schmeichel in June 2011?
Leeds United

2) Which central midfielder arrived at the club from Manchester United in January 2012?
Danny Drinkwater

3) Future title winning captain Wes Morgan was signed from which club in January 2012?
Nottingham Forest

4) May 2012 saw the arrival of Jamie Vardy who was bought from which team?
Fleetwood Town

5) Striker Chris Wood was transferred from which side in January 2013?
West Brom

6) Defender Matt Mills left the club to sign for which team in July 2012?
Bolton Wanderers

7) From which French side was Riyad Mahrez bought in January 2014?
Le Havre

8) Which striker arrived on a free from Crystal Palace in January 2014?
Kevin Phillips

9) Which striker left Leicester in July 2013 to sign for Bolton Wanderers?
Jermaine Beckford

10) From which Italian side was Esteban Cambiasso signed in the summer of 2014?
Inter Milan

11) Which future title winning right back arrived from QPR in August 2014?
Danny Simpson

12) From where was Robert Huth bought in June 2015?

Stoke City

13) Striker Shinji Okazaki came in from which German club in 2015?

Mainz

14) Which central midfielder was brought in from Napoli in August 2015?

Goekhan Inler

15) Who did David Nugent sign for after leaving Leicester in 2015?

Middlesbrough

16) Jeffrey Schlupp was sold to which team in the January transfer window of 2017?

Crystal Palace

17) Which centre back was bought from Hull City in June 2017?

Harry Maguire

18) Ricardo Pereira joined the club from which Portuguese side in June 2018?
Porto

19) Ron-Robert Zieler left Leicester in July 2017, joining which German team?
Stuttgart

20) Which player was bought from Freiburg in the summer of 2018?
Caglar Soyuncu

21) Who was sold to Villarreal in January 2019?
Vicente Iborra

22) Which midfielder arrived from Monaco in July 2019?
Youri Tielemans

23) From which Italian side was Dennis Praet bought in the summer of 2019?
Sampdoria

Cup Games – Answers

1) Leicester won the League Cup in the year 2000 after winning 2-1 over Tranmere Rovers thanks to a brace from which player?
Matt Elliott

2) Wycombe shocked Leicester in the 2001 FA Cup Quarter Final when which player scored a late winner for the lower league side?
Roy Essandoh

3) Who hit a hat-trick as Leicester hammered Nottingham Forest 4-0 in the FA Cup Third Round in January 2012?
Jermaine Beckford

4) Which team beat Leicester 6-0 in the League Cup Third Round in October 2001?
Leeds United

5) Who scored the late winner as Manchester United beat the foxes 2-1 in the 2016 Community Shield?
Zlatan Ibrahimovic

6) Which side knocked Leicester out of the 2000/01 UEFA Cup in the First Round?
Red Star Belgrade

7) Who opened the scoring in Leicester's opening game of the 2016/17 Champions League Group Stage versus Club Brugge?
Marc Albrighton

8) Which team did Leicester knock out at the Last 16 stage of the 2016/17 Champions League?
Sevilla

9) Leicester lost 9-8 on penalties to which side in the 2011/12 League Cup Third Round?
Cardiff City

10) Which team beat Leicester on aggregate in the 2019/20 League Cup Semi Final?
Aston Villa

11) Which lower league side beat Leicester in the Third Round of the FA Cup in 2019?
Newport County

12) Leicester were beaten on penalties in the Quarter Finals of the League Cup in both 2017 and 2018 by which team?
Manchester City

First Goals II – Answers

1) Ben Chilwell
   Tottenham Hotspur

2) Harry Maguire
   Brighton

3) Kelechi Iheanacho
   Manchester United

4) Youri Tielemans
   Fulham

5) James Maddison
   Wolverhampton Wanderers

6) Matty Fryatt
   Cardiff City

7) Matt Oakley
   Cheltenham Town

8) Steve Howard
   Coventry City

9) Lloyd Dyer
   Cheltenham Town

10) Darius Vassell
    Doncaster Rovers

11) Marc Albrighton
    Chelsea

12) Hamza Choudhury
    Newcastle United

13) James Justin
    Luton Town

Premier League Title – Answers

1) Who scored the equaliser for Chelsea to secure a 2-2 draw with Tottenham in May 2016 which handed the Premier League title to Leicester?
Eden Hazard

2) Who scored Leicester's goal as they secured an important 1-1 draw at Old Trafford in May 2016?
Wes Morgan

3) Who headed in the winner as Spurs were beaten 1-0 away from home in January 2016?
Robert Huth

4) Who inflicted Leicester's first loss on them in September 2015?
Arsenal

5) Leicester beat Newcastle 1-0 in March 2016, who scored the only goal of the game with an overhead kick?
Shinji Okazaki

6) Who was sent off in the dramatic 2-1 loss to Arsenal in February 2016?
Danny Simpson

7) Who scored the February 2016 goal of the month against Liverpool?
Jamie Vardy

8) Jamie Vardy scored in 11 Premier League games in a row by netting against Manchester United, but who provided the assist?
Christian Fuchs

9) Who scored a brace in the 3-1 win away at Manchester City in February 2016?
Robert Huth

10) Which player netted the late equaliser for Leicester from the penalty spot against West Ham after Jamie Vardy had been sent off in April 2016?
Leonardo Ulloa

11) Which player scored a late winner on his Leicester debut in the 3-2 comeback win over Aston Villa in September 2015?
Nathan Dyer

12) Which team did Leicester face in their last home game of the 2015/16 season?
Everton

Printed in Great Britain
by Amazon

13049358R00037